ISBN 978-1-331-37125-0
PIBN 10180666

MANDATORY JOINT RETURNS

Joint Income Tax Returns

THE PROVISION

The bill as reported by your committee requires husbands and wives living together to file a joint return if their aggregate gross income is $2,000 or over and to compute the tax on the aggregate income. The liability for the tax may be joint and several or, at the election of either spouse, may be apportioned between them. The apportionment is to be made according to the ratio of the taxes which each spouse would have been required to pay had they filed separate returns. An example is attached to the appendix showing how the apportionment rule is applied.

NECESSITY FOR THE PROVISION

(1) Entire income earned by one spouse.

Under the present law, if the entire income is earned by the husband, the family is required to pay a greater tax than if the wife had contributed to the family income. For example, if the husband and wife had an income of $10,000 per year but it was all earned by the husband, the tax under the present law with the proposed rates in the bill will amount to $1,166. On the other hand, if $5,000 of the income was contributed by the wife, the total tax to be paid by the family under the present law with the proposed rates will be $880, or $440 by each spouse. These two families have exactly the same income, yet one will pay $286 more than the other. Since in most cases, the family income is contributed by the husband, the present law operates unjustly against the great majority of families in the country. The man whose wife has a separate income is in a better position than the man whose wife has no separate income. In the former case, he does not have to set aside as much of his earnings to provide for his wife as in the latter case, yet the existing law actually favors the more fortunate family.

(2) Husbands and wives living in different sections of the country.

The present law permits a family living in one section of the country to pay a lesser tax than a family living in another section of the country. For example, if the husband is a resident of California and earns a salary of $10,000 a year, this salary is divided equally between husband and wife for income-tax purposes. On the other hand, if the husband was living in New York or some other non-community-property State, he is required to report his entire salary as his own for Federal-income tax purposes. The husband in the non-community-property State has no means of mitigating this burden, for the reason that the Supreme Court has held (*Lucas* v. *Earl*, 281 U. S. 111) that an assignment of income for personal services is not recognized for Federal income-tax purposes.   In commenting upon this inequity, Mark Graves, commissioner of taxation and finance, Albany, N. Y., stated in a letter to Congressman Reed, of New York, inserted in the joint hearings on tax evasion and avoidance, 1937, page 37:

A family living in a non-community-property State, having an income of a certain size, should, in all fairness, contribute as much to the support of the Federal Government as does a like family with the same income in any other State.

(3) Family receiving entire income from earnings.

The present law also discriminates against a family living in a non-community-property State receiving all or the greater part of the income from earnings as contrasted with a family receiving all or the greater part of the income from investments.   Husbands and wives frequently transfer property between each other, thus splitting up their income for tax purposes.   As previously pointed out, an assignment of earned income is not recognized for Federal income-tax purposes.

(4) Option to file separate returns.

The present law by permitting husbands and wives to file separate returns or joint returns at their own option always operates to the disadvantage of the Government and in favor of the taxpayers.   If each has income of any considerable size, each will ordinarily make a separate return, in order to reduce their income taxes.   If the husband and wife can so arrange their affairs that the wife is in receipt of a portion of the income, income taxes can be considerably reduced, especially in the case of the larger taxpayers.   The lawbooks are filled with cases where the husband and wife have split up their incomes for the purpose of avoiding the progressive income-tax schedule.

ADVANTAGES OF THE COMMITTEE PROPOSAL

It was the opinion of your committee that division of income between husband and wife as a tax-saving device has no equitable basis. It results in an unequal distribution of the tax burden as between families similarly situated.   The joint return proposal will overcome the inequities referred to and will result in a more equitable distribution of the tax burden.   It appears proper to treat husbands and wives as a taxable unit for purposes of the Federal income tax.   The proposal has the following virtues:

(1) It prevents the income-tax law from operating unfairly with respect to a family where all the income is received by one spouse as compared with a family where the income is received by both.

(2) It removes the discrimination under the present law against earned income in favor of investment income.

(3) It treats a family living in one part of the United States in the same manner as a family living in another part of the United States, thus removing the discrimination at present existing in favor of those residing in community-property States.

(4) It does not invade the rights of a married woman.   It treats her exactly in the same manner as her husband for Federal tax purposes.   It merely regards the marital community as the taxable unit instead of the individuals who make it up.

(5) The inherent property rights of the separate members of the taxable unit are in no way invaded.   The proposal merely deter-

mines the amount of tax to be paid by the unit and permits the tax so determined to be apportioned on an equitable basis.

(6) It prevents the income tax from being avoided through inter-spouse transfers. Property acquired by one spouse may be transferred to the other spouse mainly for the purpose of reducing the tax liability of the one who would otherwise have the greater income.

(7) It is not believed that the joint return will result in any increase in the divorce rate in the United States or adversely affect the morals of American families. A compulsory joint return in Great Britain has been required for more than 20 years, and their divorce rate is not as high per capita as in the United States.

The rate of divorces by each 1,000 of population in 1935 was, in the United States, 1.71 percent as against 0.10 percent in England and Wales. The number of divorces for each thousand marriages was, in 1935, in the United States, 164 divorces for each 1,000 marriages, in England and Wales, 12 divorces for each 1,000 marriages.

(8) The mandatory joint return will not result in an increase in the tax of any family whose net income does not exceed $4,000. Where the family has one dependent, the income would have to exceed $4,400 before the joint return will result in an increase in tax. For every additional dependent, the net income would have to be increased by $400, before the joint return would result in any increase in tax.

(9) The proposal levies the tax according to ability to pay. The taxable capacity is made to depend upon the income that accrued to the marital community and not upon the way that income happens fortuitously to be owned by members of the union. In the majority of cases where the wife has separate income, she contributes to the common purse, either by actual merger of her income with her husband's or by bearing expenses which in less fortunate households falls upon the husband.

CONSTITUTIONALITY OF PROPOSAL

It seems clear that Congress has the constitutional power to enact this proposed amendment. Generically an income tax is classed as an excise (*Brushaber* v. *Union Pac. R. R.*, 240 U. S. 1). The only express constitutional limitation upon such taxes is that they be geographically uniform. The only other possible limitations upon this kind of exercise of the taxing power are those imposed by the broad outlines of the due process clause of the fifth amendment. Obviously the proposed amendment does not run counter to the constitutional mandate of uniformity. With respect to the possible application of the due process clause, the problem revolves essentially around the power of Congress to classify income for purposes of taxation. May Congress place married persons who live together in a separate class and, by reason of the fact that each one of those persons has a separate income, require each of them to pay a higher tax upon his or her income than he or she would have been required to pay had they lived separately?

The Supreme Court has indicated the scope of the power of Congress in this regard in the following language:

In levying excise taxes the most ample authority has been recognized from the beginning to select some and omit other possible subjects of taxation, to select one calling and omit another, to tax one class of property and to forbear to tax another (*Flint* v. *Stone Tracy Co.*, 220 U. S. 107, 158).

Applying this principle specifically to income taxes, it has always been recognized that Congress has plenary authority to classify income for purposes of taxation, and in fact Congress has frequently exercised this authority. For example, in *Flint* v. *Stone Tracy Co.,* *supra,* the Court sustained the power of Congress to levy a tax on income derived from doing business in corporate form although persons who derived income from exactly the same kind of business were not subject to tax if they did not carry on that business in the corporate form. Under the Revenue Act of 1913, a single person was allowed an exemption of $3,000 but married persons living together were entitled to an exemption of only $4,000. If the husband and wife were separated and living apart from each other, each was entitled to an exemption of $3,000. It was contended in the *Brushaber* *case, supra,* that "want of due process" arises from the provisions of the act allowing a deduction for the purpose of ascertaining the taxable income of stated amounts on the ground that the provisions discriminate between married and single people and discriminates between husbands and wives who are living together and those who are not. In denying this contention, the Court said:

' * * * So far as the due process clause of the fifth amendment is relied upon, it suffices to say that there is no basis for such reliance since it is equally well settled that such clause is not a limitation upon the taxing power conferred upon Congress by the Constitution; in other words, that the Constitution does not conflict with itself by conferring upon the one hand a taxing power and taking the same power away on the other by the limitations of the due process clause (*Treat* v. *White,* 181 U. S. 264; *Patton* v. *Brady,* 184 U. S. 608; *McCray* v. *United States,* 195 U. S. 27, 61; *Flint* v. *Stone Tracy Co., supra; Billings* v. *United States,* 232, U. S. 261, 282). And no change in the situation here would arise even if it be conceded, as we think it must be, that this doctrine would have no application in a case where although there was a seeming exercise of the taxing power, the act complained of was so arbitrary as to constrain to the conclusion that it was not the exertion of taxation but a confiscation of property, that is, a taking of the same in violation of the fifth amendment, or, what is equivalent thereto, was so wanting in basis for classification as to produce such a gross and patent inequality as to inevitably lead to the same conclusion. We say this because none of the propositions relied upon in the remotest degree present such questions. * * * In fact, comprehensively surveying all the contentions relied upon, aside from the erroneous construction of the amendment which we have previously disposed of, we cannot escape the conclusion that they all rest upon the mistaken theory that although there be differences between the subjects taxed, to differently tax them transcends the limit of taxation and amounts to a want of due process, and that where a tax levied is believed by one who resists its enforcement to be wanting in wisdom and to operate injustice, from that fact in the nature of things there arises a want of due process of law and a resulting authority in the judiciary to exceed its powers and correct what is assumed to be mistaken or unwise exertions by the legislative authority of its lawful powers, even although there be no semblance of warrant in the Constitution for so doing.

More recently the Court has sustained the power of Congress to classify income for the purposes of taxation in *United States* v. *Hudson* (299 U. S. 498), and in *Helvering* v. *Northwest Steel Mills* (311 U. S. 46). In the *Hudson case* the Court sustained a special income tax of 50 percent on the profits derived from the transfer of interests in silver bullion. In the *Northwest Steel Mills* case the Court sustained the surtax imposed upon undistributed corporate earnings by the Revenue Act of 1936. A still more striking example is the recent tax on unjust enrichment, imposed by the Revenue Act of 1936, which levies a tax of 80 percent upon special kinds of income. These illustrations amply demonstrate the power of Congress to classify income for taxation purposes.

Coming down to the classification made by the proposed amendments, it should be noted that the proposed levy does not change the fundamental liabilities of the parties. Each spouse is required to pay a tax only upon his or her separate income. There is no imposition of a liability upon one person for the taxes payable by another; there is only an increase of tax upon the individual income of each spouse. Primarily a tax is a forced contribution from the members of a society to provide the necessary funds for the functioning of that society as an integrated unit. In levying a graduated income tax, Congress has given recognition to the principle that these forced exactions should be levied upon various individuals with reference to their ability to pay. In pursuance of this principle, Congress has from the beginning recognized the family status as sufficiently singular to permit of special treatment. Thus the provision of the present law which allows a man to take a deduction from his gross income for dependents is merely a recognition that this man's ability to pay is not as great as that of the man who has no dependents and therefore the tax liability of the former is reduced.

From 1913 on Congress has provided such special treatment for the head of a family. Conversely, if Congress in the exercise of its judgment concludes that a man's ability to pay a higher tax is materially affected by the fact that other people in his economic unit—the family—have incomes of their own, then it may take that factor into consideration in fixing the tax such a man should pay. Thus Congress has declared that deductions may not be taken for losses resulting from sales of property between members of the same family. See section 24 (a) (6) of the Revenue Acts of 1934 and 1936 and section 24 (b) (1) (A) of the Revenue Act of 1938. Clearly Congress is not limited in classification for the imposition of higher taxes to a consideration of the amount of income only. It has been demonstrated that it may consider as a factor in classification the particular kind of source of the income. It has also been shown that Congress has always considered as a factor in classification the ability of the taxpayer to pay as affected by his family obligations. A man whose wife enjoys an independent income may as a practical matter be thereby relieved from sufficient familial burdens to materially increase his ability to support the Government. For example a man in such a position is not under the same practical burden to provide insurance for his wife in case of his death as the man whose wife has no independent income; or he may be relieved from the burden of providing her with numerous small luxuries from his own income if she is able to purchase those things for herself. It has often been said by the Supreme Court that taxation is essentially a practical matter. Congress may therefore take into consideration the practicalities of the situation and classify accordingly.

The only authority against the constitutionality of the proposed legislation is *Hoeper* v. *Tax Commission* (284 U. S. 206). There the State of Wisconsin had provided for treatment of spouses who enjoyed independent incomes similar to that provided for in the proposed amendments. There was, however, one essential difference. Under the Wisconsin law each person whose income was included within the tax computation was liable for the entire tax. The Supreme Court held that this legislation was unconstitutional on the ground that each person was liable for the total tax and therefore A was required

to pay a tax on B's income.   But this conclusion was reached over
the vigorous dissent of Mr. Justice Holmes, Mr. Justice Brandeis,
and Mr. Justice Stone, and the views of the dissenters in the *Hoeper
case* have recently been measurably strengthened by the Supreme
Court in a series of significant decisions.   *Burnet* v. *Wells* (289 U. S.
670), *Helvering* v. *Clifford* (309 U. S. 331), see also *Helvering* v. *Horst*
(311 U. S. 112), *Helvering* v. *Eubank* (311 U. S. 122), *Hormel* v.
Helvering (85 L. Ed. 651), *Harrison* v. *Schaffner* (85 L. Ed. 694).

These cases conclusively demonstrate that the convenient phrase,
"A may not be taxed on B's" income, is by no means an all-pervasive
formula which will assist in the solution of tax problems.   On the
contrary A may be taxed on B's income if there are sufficient justifi-
catory facts.   The inquiry does not cease with a determination that
A is being taxed on income which he did not receive, but must be
further pursued with a view to discovering whether there are sufficient facts to so justify taxing A.   The *Wells, Clifford, Horst, Eubank,
Hormel,* and *Schaffner cases* are examples of situations in which the
Supreme Court has concluded that A could be so taxed.

Thus in the *Wells case* the taxpayer had created certain irrevocable
trusts the income from which was used to pay premiums on policies
of insurance on his life.   The Court held that the provision of the
Revenue Act of 1924 which directed that such income be taxed to
the grantor was constitutional, saying, through Mr. Justice Cardozo
(pp. 677–679):

> The controversy is one as to the boundaries of legislative power.   It must be
> dealt with in a large way, as questions of due process always are, not narrowly or
> pedantically, in slavery to forms or phrases.   "Taxation is not so much concerned
> with the refinements of title as it is with the actual command over the property
> taxed—the actual benefit for which the tax is paid" (*Corliss* v. *Bowers, supra,*
> p. 378; cf. *Burnet* v. *Guggenheim, supra,* p. 283).   Refinements of title have at
> times supplied the rule when the question has been one of construction and
> nothing more, a question as to the meaning of a taxing act to be read in favor of
> the taxpayer.   Refinements of title are without controlling force when a statute,
> unmistakable in meaning, is assailed by a taxpayer as overpassing the bounds of
> reason, an exercise by the lawmakers of arbitrary power.   In such circumstances
> the question is no longer whether the concept of ownership reflected in the statute
> is to be squared with the concept embodied, more or less vaguely, in common-law
> traditions.   The question is whether it is one that an enlightened legislator might
> act upon without affront to justice.   Even administrative convenience, the practi-
> cal necessities of an efficient system of taxation, will have heed and recognition
> within reasonable limits (*Milliken* v. *United States,* 283 U. S. 15, 24, 25; *Reinecke*
> v. *Smith, supra*).   Liability does not have to rest upon the enjoyment by the
> taxpayer of all the privileges and benefits enjoyed by the most favored owner at a
> given time or place (*Corliss* v. *Bowers, supra; Reinecke* v. *Smith, supra*).   Govern-
> ment in casting about for proper subjects of taxation is not confined by the tradi-
> tional classification of interests or estates.   It may tax not only ownership but
> any right or privilege that is a constituent of ownership (*Nashville, C. & St. L. Ry.
> Co.* v. *Wallace,* 288 U. S. 249, 268; *Bromley* v. *McCaughn,* 280 U. S. 124, 136).
> Liability may rest upon the enjoyment by the taxpayer of privileges and benefits
> so substantial and important as to make it reasonable and just to deal with him
> as if he were the owner, and to tax him on that basis.   A margin must be allowed
> for the play of legislative judgment.   To overcome this statute the taxpayer
> must show that in attributing to him the ownership of the income of the trusts, or
> something fairly to be dealt with as equivalent to ownership, the lawmakers have
> done a wholly arbitrary thing, have found equivalence where there was none nor
> anything approaching it, and laid a burden unrelated to privilege or bene-
> fit.   * * *

In *Helvering* v. *Clifford, supra,* the Court pointed out that the
familial relationship has sufficient individuality to have a substantial
effect upon tax consequences.   In that case a husband had created a
trust of certain securities for the term of 5 years, the income from which

was to be paid to his wife. In holding the husband taxable upon the income of that trust,[1] the Court said (pp. 335–336):

We have at best a temporary reallocation of income within an intimate family group. Since the income remains in the family and since the husband retains control over the investment, he has rather complete assurance that the trust will not effect any substantial change in his economic position. It is hard to imagine that respondent felt himself the poorer after this trust had been executed or, if he did, that it had any rational foundation in fact, for as a result of the terms of the trust and the intimacy of the familial relationship respondent retained the substance of full enjoyment of all the rights which previously he had in the property. That might not be true if only strictly legal rights were considered, but when the benefits flowing to him indirectly through the wife are added to the legal rights he retained, the aggregate may be said to be a fair equivalent of what he previously had. To exclude from the aggregate those indirect benefits would be to deprive section 22 (a) of considerable vitality and to treat as immaterial what may be highly relevant considerations in the creation of such family trusts, for where the head of the household has income in excess of normal needs, it may well make but little difference to him (except income-tax-wise) where portions of that income are routed—so long as it stays in the family group.

Not only does the *Hoeper case* have no authority in the field of Federal income taxation, but its vitality as an effective limitation upon the taxing power of the States has also been dissipated by more recent decisions of the Supreme Court which have seriously undermined its foundations by holding that a State is not forbidden by the fourteenth amendment to make such classifications as the legislature regards to be necessary to protect its revenues. In *Madden* v. *Kentucky* (309 U. S. 83), the Supreme Court upheld a Kentucky statute which taxed deposits in banks outside of the State at 50 cents per $100, although deposits in banks within the State were taxed at only 10 cents per $100. The Court there said (pp. 87–88):

The broad discretion as to classification possessed by a legislature in the field of taxation has long been recognized. * * * Traditionally classification has been a device for fitting tax programs to local needs and usages in order to achieve an equitable distribution of the tax burden. It has, because of this, been pointed out that in taxation, even more than in other fields, legislatures possess the greatest freedom in classification Since the members of a legislature necessarily enjoy a familiarity with local conditions which this Court cannot have, the presumption of constitutionality can be overcome only by the most explicit demonstration that a classification is a hostile and oppressive discrimination against particular persons and classes. The burden is on the one attacking the legislative arrangement to negative every conceivable basis which might support it.

It may fairly be predicted that if the Supreme Court were presented today with the question presented in the *Hoeper case* that that case would not be followed. But even if the *Hoeper case* be taken at its face value, the proposed amendments do not come within its scope. The motivating factor for the decision in that case was the provision that each person whose income was included within the tax computation was liable for the entire tax. It has been pointed out that the legislation here under consideration does not make the spouses jointly and severally liable for the entire tax unless they so elect. Each person is required to pay a tax only upon his own income and not upon the income of any other person. The net effect is merely that the amount of the tax which he is required to pay is conditioned by the fact that he lives in an economic unit which has other income accruing to it.

For these reasons it is concluded that it is within the power of Congress to make the suggested changes in the Internal Revenue Code.

---

[1] Though the taxpayer argued on the basis of the *Hoeper case* that it was unconstitutional to tax A on B's income, the Court did not even deem it necessary to discuss the point.

Appendix I

EXAMPLE OF APPLICATION OF COMMITTEE PROPOSAL

The liability for the tax is to be joint and several unless one spouse elects to have such liability apportioned between the spouses. The allocation of the tax between the spouses is to be upon that portion of the income of the marital community which bears the same ratio to such tax as the tax for which such spouse would be liable in the event he were required to file a separate return to the sum of the separate taxes. In computing the separate tax for the purpose of the allocation, each spouse is deemed to have a personal exemption of $1,000 and the credit for dependents is to be computed as if husband and wife were single persons. The following example will show how the section operates:

Husband's gross income		$11, 000. 00
Wife's gross income		114, 000. 00
Total gross income		125, 000. 00
Total deductions		15, 000. 00
Combined net income		110, 000. 00
Credits:		
Earned income	$2, 400 00	
Personal exemption	2, 000. 00	
Total credits		4, 400. 00
Net income in excess of credits for normal tax purpose		105, 600. 00
Normal tax at 4 percent		4, 224. 00
Surtax on $108,000		50, 780. 00
Total normal and surtax		55, 004. 00
Plus defense tax, 10 percent of ($54,996) difference between net income and total normal and surtax, or		5, 499. 60
Total tax under committee bill		60, 503. 60
Allocation of tax liability:		
Husband's tax computed separately:		
Gross income		11, 000. 00
Deductions		1, 000. 00
Net income		10, 000. 00
Credits:		
Earned income	$1, 000. 00	
Personal exemption	1, 000. 00	
Total credits		2, 000. 00
Net income in excess of credits for normal tax purpose		8, 000. 00
Normal tax at 4 percent		320. 00
Surtax on $9,000		970. 00
Total normal and surtax		1, 290. 00
Plus 10-percent defense tax		129. 00
Total tax, husband computed separately		1, 419. 00

Allocation of tax liability—Continued.
Wife's tax computed separately:

Gross income	$114, 000. 00
Deductions	14, 000. 00
Net income	100, 000. 00

Credits:

Earned income	$1, 400. 00	
Personal exemption	1, 000. 00	
Total credits		2, 400. 00
Net income in excess of credits for normal tax purpose		97, 600. 00
Normal tax at 4 percent		3, 904. 00
Surtax on $99,000		45, 210. 00
Total normal and surtax		49, 114. 00
Plus 10 percent defense tax		4, 911. 40
Total tax, wife computed separately		54, 025. 40
Combined tax of husband and wife computed separately		55, 444. 40

Percent of combined tax (separate returns):
Husband, 2.559 percent.
Wife, 97.441 percent.
Husband's and wife's tax liability under joint return:

Husband, 2.559 percent of $60,403.60	1, 548. 29
Wife, 97.441 percent of $60,403.60	58, 955. 31
Total tax under joint return	60, 503. 60

APPENDIX II.

Comparison of tax on married person under Joint Return, with tax computed under separate returns, on specified net incomes (all income earned)

Combined net income	Under joint return	Under separate returns — Percentage of combined net income attributable to each spouse					
		Husband 90 / Wife 10	80 / 20	75 / 25	70 / 30	60 / 40	50 / 50
$2,500	$38.50	$38.50	$38.50	$38.50	$38.50	$38.50	$38.50
$3,000	85.80	85.80	85.80	85.80	85.80	85.80	85.80
$4,000	180.40	180.40	180.40	180.40	180.40	180.40	180.40
$5,000	308.00	291.50	275.00	275.00	275.00	275.00	275.00
$6,000	435.60	415.80	396.00	386.10	376.20	369.60	369.60
$7,000	596.20	550.00	517.00	505.45	497.20	497.20	497.20
$8,000	756.80	704.00	661.20	624.80	624.80	624.80	624.80
$9,000	961.40	862.40	798.60	777.15	762.30	752.40	752.40
$10,000	1,166.00	1,056.00	946.00	929.50	913.00	880.00	880.00
$15,000	2,545.40	2,227.50	1,980.80	1,889.25	1,815.00	1,727.00	1,727.00
$20,000	4,338.40	3,757.60	3,308.80	3,150.40	2,992.00	2,838.00	2,838.00
$25,000	6,505.40	5,625.40	4,943.40	4,673.90	4,464.90	4,217.40	4,180.00
$30,000	8,936.40	7,768.20	6,798.00	6,444.90	6,168.80	5,803.60	5,728.80
$50,000	20,002.40	17,659.40	15,866.40	15,238.40	14,715.80	14,088.80	13,956.80
$60,000	26,206.40	23,210.00	21,049.60	20,270.80	19,676.80	19,016.80	18,884.80
$80,000	39,318.40	35,125.20	32,326.80	31,358.80	30,676.80	29,774.80	29,532.80
$100,000	53,310.40	47,876.40	44,470.80	43,414.80	42,600.80	41,544.80	41,192.80
$150,000	88,299.60	81,106.00	77,428.00	76,199.50	75,138.80	73,664.80	73,288.80
$250,000	159,013.60	148,665.00	144,622.00	143,727.20	143,162.00	143,040.00	143,087.20
$500,000	346,905.60	329,696.00	324,982.00	323,679.20	322,329.20	320,115.20	319,251.20
$750,000	540,637.60	519,718.00	513,775.20	511,075.20	508,600.20	505,243.20	504,379.20
$1,000,000	736,519.60	712,860.00	704,357.20	700,775.20	698,825.20	695,825.20	694,943.20
$2,000,000	1,529,501.60	1,495,539.20	1,483,839.20	1,481,139.20	1,479,339.20	1,476,189.20	1,474,407.20
$5,000,000	3,935,483.60	3,882,621.20	3,871,371.20	3,869,121.20	3,866,835.20	3,862,371.20	3,862,371.20

APPENDIX III

Joint returns filed by States, and estimated additional joint returns which would have been filed in 1938 if mandatory joint returns had been required of husbands and wives living together.

State	Number of joint returns filed	Estimated [1] additional mandatory joint returns	Total joint returns	Percent of mandatory joint returns to total number of joint returns
Alabama	21,073	768	21,841	3.52
Arizona	9,849	1,261	11,110	11.35
Arkansas	12,368	383	12,751	3.00
California	213,009	28,580	241,589	11.83
Colorado	21,059	939	21,998	4.27
Connecticut	48,673	3,532	52,205	6.77
Delaware	7,482	684	8,166	8.38
District of Columbia	41,170	2,502	43,672	5.73
Florida	30,835	2,133	32,968	6.47
Georgia	31,947	1,374	33,321	4.12
Hawaii	8,783	508	9,291	5.47
Idaho	5,887	856	6,743	12.69
Illinois	228,240	10,273	238,513	4.31
Indiana	59,335	1,982	61,317	3.23
Iowa	39,750	1,223	40,973	2.98
Kansas	29,450	1,003	30,453	3.29
Kentucky	24,529	1,347	25,876	5.21
Louisiana	25,054	5,199	30,253	17.19
Maine	12,051	665	12,716	5.23
Maryland	64,307	3,175	67,482	4.70
Massachusetts	115,938	8,596	124,534	6.90
Michigan	132,080	4,621	136,701	3.38
Minnesota	50,283	2,033	52,316	3.89
Mississippi	11,494	462	11,956	3.86
Missouri	69,004	3,033	72,037	4.21
Montana	13,035	275	13,310	2.07
Nebraska	21,527	665	22,192	3.00
Nevada	3,878	459	4,337	10.58
New Hampshire	8,982	546	9,528	5.73
New Jersey	139,331	6,740	146,071	4.61
New Mexico	6,823	646	7,469	8.65
New York	485,084	26,977	512,061	5.27
North Carolina	26,727	1,496	28,223	5.30
North Dakota	6,573	156	6,729	2.32
Ohio	160,061	6,282	166,343	3.78
Oklahoma	32,542	1,680	34,222	4.91
Oregon	24,931	804	25,735	3.12
Pennsylvania	261,722	9,518	271,240	3.51
Rhode Island	16,418	872	17,290	5.04
South Carolina	12,890	539	13,429	4.01
South Dakota	6,402	149	6,551	2.27
Tennessee	29,758	1,097	30,855	3.56
Texas	99,248	17,267	116,515	14.82
Utah	10,702	361	11,063	3.26
Vermont	5,643	231	5,874	3.93
Virginia	36,731	1,377	38,108	3.61
Washington [2]	43,425	5,942	49,367	12.04
West Virginia	25,657	880	26,537	3.32
Wisconsin	68,191	3,025	71,216	4.25
Wyoming	6,095	178	6,273	2.84
Total	2,866,026	175,294	3,041,320	5.76

[1] Estimated on basis of number of separate returns filed by husbands and wives living together, as shown by Statistics of Income, 1938.
[2] Includes Alaska.

APPENDIX **IV**   ·

PRIOR ADVOCACY OF JOINT RETURN

When the Hill subcommittee met in 1933 to consider "income-tax loopholes," one of the issues raised was that of community property. As I recall, the staff offered a proposal to tax the income to the spouse having management and control of the property. This proposal was defeated in the subcommittee by a very close vote. The subcommittee in its report said:

> The income tax situation existing in eight States of the Union having community-property laws has been carefully considered. No recommendation in regard thereto is made by your subcommittee in view of the legal difficulties involved.

The full committee held public hearings on the subcommittee report. At that time, Dr. Magill appeared, representing the Treasury Department. In this connection, he stated:

> Under the present law, a husband and wife living together may, at their own option, make separate returns or may make a single joint return. If each has an income of any considerable size, each will ordinarily make a separate return, in order to reduce the normal tax, and, more particularly, the surtaxes which would otherwise be payable. The family income is in fact frequently expended and otherwise treated as a unit; nevertheless, if the husband and wife can so arrange their affairs that the wife is in receipt of a portion of the family income, income taxes can be considerably reduced. In other words, the present privilege of filing separate returns operates to that extent to defeat the progressive rate schedule, particularly in the case of the larger taxpayers. * * *
>
> The Treasury Department therefore recommends that the committee consider whether a husband and wife living together should not be required to file a single joint return, each to pay the tax attributable to his share of the income. Such a provision has long been in force in other countries.
>
> Reference may be made in this connection to the *Hoeper case* (284 U. S. 206), in which the Supreme Court held that a somewhat similar provision in the Wisconsin income-tax statute was invalid. The case is not, however, conclusive for two reasons. In the first place, the Wisconsin law was evidently interpreted by the Court as requiring that the husband should pay the tax on his wife's income. This objection can be eliminated by proper draftsmanship specifying otherwise. In the second place, the Federal Government is not under the same constitutional restrictions as the States in this respect.

In the 1934 hearings (p. 116), Mr. Magill stated in answer to a question by Mr. Cooper as to the status of the law:

> My own view is that a provision of this kind is so fair that the likelihood is that the court will uphold it, and I don't see anything in these decisions which would prevent them from so holding.

Dr. Magill, as the representative of the Treasury, in his testimony before the Tax Evasion and Avoidance Committee in 1937, said:

> In his statement to the Committee on Ways and Means the Acting Secretary also pointed out that the problem of taxing the incomes of spouses has a broader aspect than that of eliminating the discrimination in favor of husbands and wives living together in community-property States. Since spouses living together in non-community-property States may file separate returns, there is a strong incentive for them to arrange their property holdings in such a way as to realize the greatest possible tax advantage through a division of income or an allocation of losses (p. 310).

And then in answer to the remedy for this situation, Dr. Magill said:

> I do not know whether we have got anything essentially different from what was worked out in 1933 and 1934 or not. I have not been able to go over that carefully in the last 2 or 3 weeks. As I say, our net suggestion is that we think it would be desirable over the country as a whole to provide that the incomes of husbands and wives living together should be aggregated and the tax computed with respect to the total (p. 312.)

Appendix V

REPORT OF THE ROYAL COMMISSION ON THE INCOME TAX, 1920

Section VII. The Assessment of Married Persons

248. The correct method of assessing married persons has received a great deal of public attention both before and since the appointment of this Commission. The matter has been freely ventilated in the press and has been raised on several occasions in the House of Commons. In the course of our inquiry a considerable volume of evidence on the subject has been presented to us, and we have examined witnesses from representative women's societies; we have also received a large number of letters in connection with this part of our investigation.

249. Speaking generally, the existing position is that husband and wife are regarded as one unit for the purpose of income tax; the income of a married woman living with her husband being deemed to be (for this purpose) the income of the husband, and the husband being responsible for the inclusion of his wife's income in his own return; but this general position is subject to two important modifications.

(a) It is in the power of either spouse to elect to be separately assessed, and if that election is made, income tax is assessed, charged, and recovered on the income of the husband and on the income of the wife as if they were not married.

(b) If a married woman earns income by her own personal labor, and her husband also earns income unconnected with his wife's business or employment, a separate claim of exemption or abatement can be made in respect of the wife's earned income—provided the joint income of husband and wife does not exceed £500.

250. The option of separate assessment referred to in (a) dates from 1914; it applies to married men equally with married women, but it does not appear to be very widely known; indeed, some of the witnesses seem to have been unaware of the existence of any such provision. The option is rarely taken advantage of, either because of this prevailing want of knowledge, or because its exercise is not in fact often desired. Although a married woman can make a separate return and be assessed separately from her husband, if she wishes it, the total of their separate liabilities to income tax, if the election is made, does not differ from the combined liability that would have arisen if the option had not been exercised. For example, if husband and wife have incomes of £2,000 and £1,000 a year respectively, and claim to be separately assessed, neither is granted exemption from supertax, but the liability attaching to an income of £3,000 is divided, and charged separately upon husband and wife in proportion to the size of their respective incomes.

251. This position does not satisfy the more extreme advocates of separate assessment; they say that husband and wife should be assessed as though they were separate taxable units—without any regard to the amount of their combined incomes. This contention has been urged upon us by many witnesses, and it forms the burden of the many letters we have received on this subject—mainly written by persons who would themselves benefit by the change proposed. By those who take this view it is claimed that the right to a completely separate assessment is an essential part of separate citizenship, and that the principle of absolute equality in regard to civil obligations

should override any principle of taxation. The statement was also made that the present method of assessment imposes a penalty on marriage.

252. On the other hand, it has been contended by several witnesses that this proposal for separate assessment of husband and wife is not reconcilable with a just view of the principle of ability to bear taxation, and that the common menage which is our general mode of social life must be considered in any equitable system of taxation. From the point of view of ability to pay those who oppose separate treatment contend that it would be an anomaly if different sums of income tax were levied on two married couples enjoying equal incomes, merely because in one case the income belonged wholly to one spouse and in the other to both. In the case of a married man with £1,000 a year unearned income, the sacrifice involved by income tax, say £187 10s., may in most households be regarded as borne equally by each spouse, a sacrifice of £93, 15s. each. If the husband and wife each have £500 a year there is no such difference in their taxable capacity as would justify a sacrifice of only £60 a year each, which is what would result from treating husband and wife as two separate units.

253. If we conceive a number of households where the wife has a varying amount of separate income, but where the total income (un-earned) of the husband and wife is the same, the anomalies that would result from the proposed method of separate assessment will be apparent. Let the total income be assumed to be £1,000.

	£	s.	d.
If the husband has the whole income, the tax paid would be	187	10	0
If the husband has £900 and the wife £100, the tax paid would be	168	15	0
If the husband has £800 and the wife £200, the tax paid wolud be	162	0	0
If the husband has £700 and the wife £300, the tax paid would be	145	2	6
If the husband has £600 and the wife £400, the tax paid would be	135	15	0
If the husband has £500 and the wife £500, the tax paid would be	120	0	0

The difference in the sums borne by the first and last of these households with identical incomes would thus be £67 10s., a result which appears to us not only inequitable but ridiculous under a system which aims at adjusting the tax in accordance with the principle of ability to pay.

254. Other witnesses referred to the fact that the income of husband and wife under the ordinary conditions of married life is treated as a joint one so far as expenditure is concerned, and argued that it is, therefore, not unfair to make their expenditure for taxation dependent upon their total resources. Under the present law and practice if the husband and wife are living apart their incomes are treated as separate subjects for assessment. It was pointed out that if the allegation is correct that joint assessment is conducive to immorality (an allegation unproved in the course of our inquiry and characterized by one of the women witnesses as being neither reasonable nor probable), the logical, even if not the practicable, remedy is to render liable to joint assessment the income of two unmarried persons living together.

255. It has been stated by the Chancelor of the Exchequer in the House of Commons that the loss which would arise from the separate assessment of husband and wife would be £20,000,000, increasing possibly to £45,000,000 in consequence of avoidance of tax by trans-fer of income from the husband to the wife. To shift a burden from

the shoulders of persons whose joint income is such that their ability to pay permits of its being equitably borne by them, and to place part of that burden, by means of an increased rate, upon the shoulders of other taxpayers, would be, in our opinion, entirely contrary to all principles of equitable assessment.

256. We feel that the demand of those who favor this change is in effect not so much a demand for separate assessment or separate recovery of tax—this they can have under the existing law—as for a diminution in income-tax liability on the ground that part of the joint income happens to belong to the wife. There are two methods of recognizing, by diminished taxation, the obligations of marriage. One is to make an allowance, a wife allowance or marriage allowance, from the joint income; this wife allowance is already granted under the present law, and we have made proposals which will in effect increase it considerably. The other method is, by a complete severance in the treatment of husband and wife for income-tax purposes, to effect a differentiation the results of which will depend entirely on the particular manner in which a given income chances to be distributed between the two members of the household. The first method, seeing that it affects every married couple, is far more likely than the second to encourage marriage.

257. It strikes us as curious that, while ignoring the joint obligation of husband and wife for the purpose of pressing their claim to entirely separate treatment, the same witnesses have asked for increases in the wife and children allowances—which are express recognitions of the joint responsibilities created by marriage. It seems to us that it would be quite illogical, under the same system of taxation, to make an allowance which recognizes the joint responsibilities of husband and wife, and at the same time to grant relief to each of the partners to the union as though they were complete strangers. If separate assessment were granted the marriage allowance should logically be abolished, and the result would be a shifting of burdens from the rich to the poor, because in the vast majority of cases the wife has either no separate income at all or a separate income less than the amount of the present marriage allowance, and far less than allowance we suggest should be made.

258. The question involved should not be regarded as a political question, but purely as one of finance and revenue, and we are satisfied that it must be decided, not on any theoretical grounds of equality of citizenship, but in accordance with the outstanding principle of "ability to pay," which we recognize as governing all questions of taxation. In the application of this principle, we must regard the social conditions of the country in which the taxation is imposed. The great majority of married persons live together and use their several incomes for common purposes, and this common menage and joint dependency is recognized, to the benefit of the wife, for other purposes of taxation, e. g., legacy and succession duties payable by a widow are less than those payable by a person unrelated to the deceased.

259. The aggregation for income-tax purposes of the income of husband and wife is not dependent upon any medieval conception of the subordination of women; nor is it a question of sex disability, since either partner can claim separate assessment and separate collection. The incomes are aggregated because the law of taxable

capacity is the supreme law in matters of taxation, and taxable capacity is, in fact, found to depend upon the amount of the income that accrues to the married pair, and not upon the way in which that income happens fortuitously to be owned by the members of the union. It is beyond question that in the immense majority of cases where the wife has separate means she contributes to the common purse, either by actual merger of her income with her husband's, or by bearing expenses which in less fortunate households fall upon the husband.

260. We have given a great deal of time and attention to this subject and have considered with the utmost care all the arguments that have been put before us, and we have been forced to the conclusion that the grievance complained of is more vocal than real, in other words, that it is a grievance rather than a hardship. We therefore recommend that *the aggregation of the incomes of wife and husband should continue to be the rule.*

261. In paragraph 249 (b) we referred to the exceptional treatment allowed under the existing law to the earned income of a married woman where the joint income does not exceed £500. The effect of this provision, in a case where, for example, husband and wife each earn £250 and have no other income, is that two abatements of £120 each are allowed, as compared with the single abatement of £100 which would be allowed if the whole £500 were earned either by the husband or by the wife. The limit of £500 has been represented to us as too low in present conditions. We agree with this point of view, and recommend that the relief in its present form should be discontinued, and that where the wife has £50 or more of earned income the joint exemption or abatement allowance to a married couple should be increased from £250 (earned) to £300 (earned). Where the wife earns less than £50, the joint allowance for a married couple should be increased from £250 (earned) by the amount of the wife's earnings.

262. In connection with this subject, our attention has been directed to some minor details in regard to which we make the following suggestions: (a) *that the revenue should have power of assessment, apportionment, and recovery of the tax against the spouses in respect of their separate incomes where necessary to the collection of the tax;* (b) *that the notice to be given by a wife or husband requiring separate assessment should be allowed to be given at any time not later than June 30 in the year of assessment;* and (c) *that when husband and wife are separately assessed any relief in respect of their unearned or investment income should be given to the husband and to the wife in proportion to their respective assessable incomes.*

CPSIA information can be obtained
at www.ICGtesting.com
Printed in the USA
BVHW071956070119
537207BV00023B/3246/P